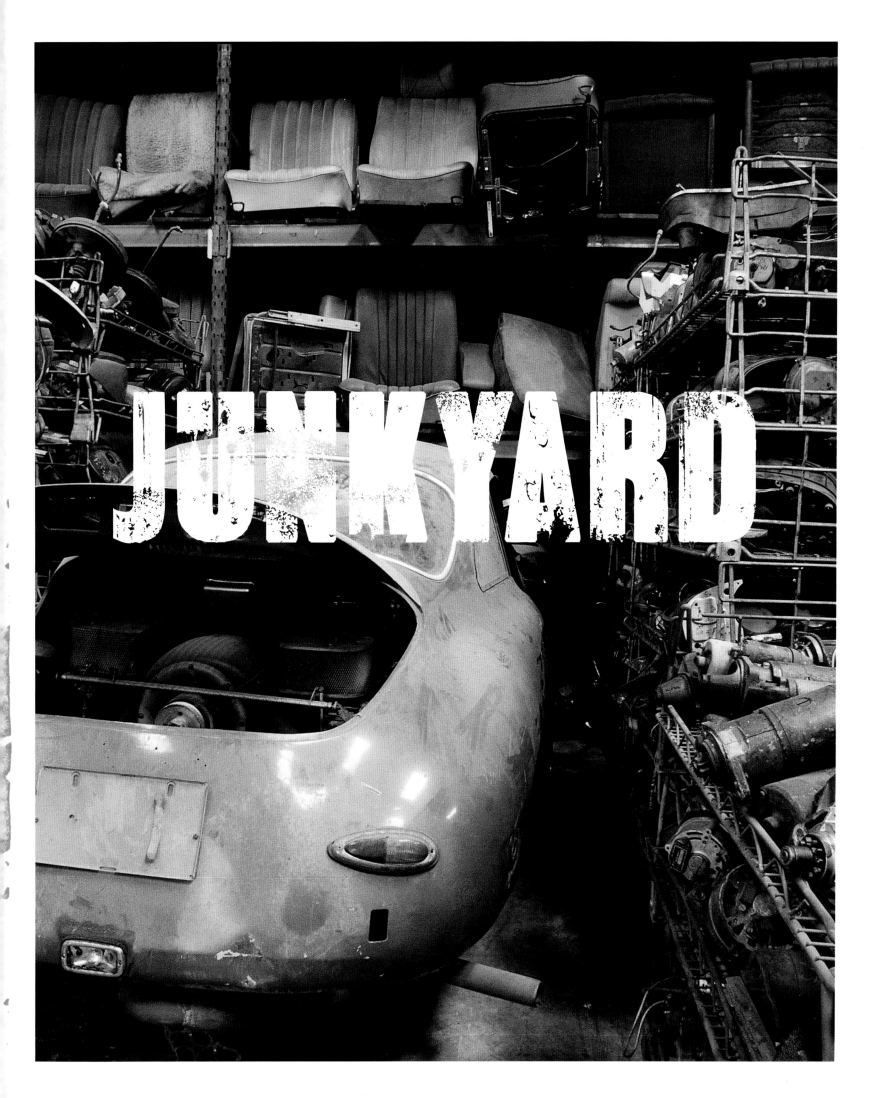

JUNKYARD

Inspiring | Educating | Creating | Entertaining

Brimming with creative inspiration, how-to projects, and useful information to enrich your everyday life, Quarto Knows is a favorite destination for those pursuing their interests and passions. Visit our site and dig deeper with our books into your area of interest: Quarto Creates, Quarto Cooks, Quarto Homes, Quarto Lives, Quarto Drives, Quarto Explores, Quarto Gifts, or Quarto Kids.

First Published in English in 2020 by Motorbooks, an imprint of The Quarto Group, 100 Cummings Center, Suite 265-D, Beverly, MA 01915, USA. T (978) 282-9590 F (978) 283-2742 QuartoKnows.com

ISBN: 978-0-7603-6768-1

Digital edition published in 2020
eISBN: 978-0-7603-6769-8

Library of Congress Cataloging-in-Publication Data is available.

Acquiring Editor: Zack Miller
Art Director: Cindy Samargia Laun
Translator: Tony Lewin
Cover Image: Dieter Rebmann
Page Layout and Design: Andrea Högerle
Additional Layout: Danielle Smith-Boldt
Photography: Dieter Rebmann

Printed in China

JUNKYARD

**BEHIND THE GATES AT CALIFORNIA'S SECRETIVE
EUROPEAN-CAR SALVAGE YARD**

Dieter Rebmann / Roland Löwisch

CONTENTS

PREFACE

It must have been one of his better days. He wasn't prickly—just a bit on the grumpy side. He wasn't too keen on Dieter Rebmann's cameras, but he didn't sling them away as scrap—something he had sometimes done with the equipment belonging to other journalists who, despite having arranged in advance to meet him, managed to get off on the wrong foot with him. He wasn't exactly talkative, but he did allow a couple of questions—which he even went so far as to answer. As I just said: Rudi Klein was having one of his better days.

This was in no small part down to good timing and the patient groundwork already put in by the Stuttgart-based photographer Rebmann. Years before we actually got there, Dieter had heard rumors from a friend and his son that a mysterious site in the Los Angeles area was being worked as a scrapyard by a German guy and that it was reserved almost exclusively for high-end cars. The yard's owner, Rudi Klein, was said to be no less a wonder—most likely because of the empire he had built up and the fact that everyone envied him. He had apparently been lied to, swindled, and robbed, all of which prompted him to—literally—begin minding his own business. But if someone sympathetic enough were to show up, there was a slight chance they could actually meet him—though this was still not any guarantee that they would be allowed to set foot in his luxury-car scrapyard, let alone poke around in its contents.

The scorching sun was high in the sky when we finally got to visit the German émigré, then aged 64, at his "Porche Foreign Auto Dismantling" establishment in Los Angeles, California. The sun's warmth helped take some of the menace out of Florence, this run-down suburb of South Central Los Angeles, and Klein was quick to recount the true story behind the "Porche" sign that hung over the near-impenetrable entrance to the site. Even in those early days of his business, he explained, the German sports-car manufacturer objected if the Porsche name was used by others in any way, especially for any kind of commercial purpose. Yet, to Klein's pragmatic way of thinking, no one could object to "Porche."

Klein had realized that we didn't want anything from him; we didn't want to strip out any parts, and we had no interest in skimming off any mementos for a few cents apiece. Instead, Rebmann just wanted to take pictures, and Klein let him do just that. He was actually pleased to allow it. This really was one of his better days.

So there we stood, utterly flabbergasted, looking out over 16,000 square meters of scrap—but what scrap! Nothing but once-magnificent cars—limousines completely stripped out, crumpled sports cars, coupes cut in half. And in the many large outbuildings, barns, and sheds, countless automotive treasures, either hastily covered up or completely unprotected, had for years been suffering the indignity of digested deposits from the pigeons feasting in this twilight world.

Rudi Klein was the kind of person whom some might describe as an oddball. Stubborn, and consistently so, but honest through and through—perhaps too honest for some. Stingy, for sure, but also towards himself. Whenever he went back to Germany, the multimillionaire preferred to stay in a small boarding house. His own home in Palos Verdes was large, but not especially luxurious, and his favorite advice to friends and acquaintances went like this: "Since you're going to get ripped off everywhere, you might as well allow yourself to be ripped off by me," meaning that if someone wants to offer me only $5,000 for a $15,000 item, I ask for $30,000. End of story!

In the early years of his business, no one wanted to buy parts from him. But as the classic-car hype began to grow, was he going to let his treasures go for laughable sums? Not him. As we talk, Rebmann snaps the shutter on his medium-format Fuji 680GX camera and the small Canon 1V, loaded with Agfa Scala S/W black-and-white transparency film.

We could have stayed there for days, but Klein eventually called a halt, inviting us to join him at a very German restaurant nearby, the

Blaskapelle, or Brass Band. Traditional Dirndls, Weisswurst, and Bavarian wheat beer to go with it—that's what he liked. He never cast off his German roots—quite the opposite, in fact: he really rejoiced in them. He would always prefer to stay in a broom cupboard rather than a five-star golf hotel, and in this gloomy corner of LA he didn't want to stand out—that's why he always stuck with his well-used Audi A8. Assuming, of course, that no one would twig that treasures totaling millions of dollars could be lurking behind those high walls and fences or among the tumbledown buildings inside.

Rudi Klein died of heart failure on October 21st, 2001. He was 65. Many of his ambitions went unfulfilled, such as the setting up of an "Accident Museum" with police cars, barriers, and a lot of scrap. And we never got to see him again, as we had planned.

Today, his two sons, Jason and Benji, run the business but do not let anyone onto the site; the compound itself is no longer the same, either. It is now smaller, the brothers having tidied things up. They are the only people who know what is still stored in the old barns and sheds. The "Porche" sign no longer hangs over the entrance, and the surrounding area has also changed dramatically as the city seeks to rid the suburb of its shabbiness. In the meantime, the sons are getting on with selling everything bit by bit, and on the internet you can still find whole cars listed. Many of the most precious cars still stand poised for their photo opportunity by the steel scaffolding and the towers of stacked-up Porsche 356s just inside that impenetrable entrance.

Even today, it stands as a reminder that, with his clear vision, his shrewdness in business, and his canny budgeting, Klein was one of the greats in the world of car collecting.

Hamburg/Stuttgart, Summer 2017

Roland Löwisch

PORCHE-WORLD
In order to avoid conflict with the manufacturer, Klein's company name included the word "Porche"—but everyone knew what it referred to.

INTRODUCTION
DESTINATION: NOSTALGIA

"Congratulations on your new baby boy—we love you"—that was the message on the Alvera family's greasy and grimy greeting card that still lay trampled in the footwell of the dark-green Maserati 3500 GT, chassis number 02089. The car had breathed its last with 57,101 kilometers on the clock; the driver had clearly done all he possibly could to avoid the crash, to judge by the brake discs and the tires. All in vain.

A few steps away from the Maserati stood a completely crumpled Porsche 356. The interior survival space was down to near zero. Long-forgotten dramas leave bizarre art forms in their wake—as with the Bentley just a couple of meters away. Its front half was completely burnt out, all the way to the springs in the seats—yet, up close, the upholstery in the rear seats still smelled of Connolly leather, and the doors still swung shut with a quality clunk, just as they did when new.

Our sense of astonishment was complete and inescapable. Scrapyards are two a penny, and there are plenty of interesting scrapyards, too. But what we'd stumbled across in this forgotten corner of Los Angeles was nothing short of our youthful fantasies stamped straight into sheet metal. A giant barn find but without the barn; a never-before-seen story of wealth and luxury demoted to rust and dust. Treasured designs reduced to their crude raw materials. Crammed close together lay dream cars side by side with wrecked classics every bit as exotic. Most were from the 1950s, 1960s, and 1970s: Rolls-Royces, innumerable Mercedes SL "Pagodas," "fintail" Mercedes of the 1960s, a couple of 190s and skeletons of 300SLs, old BMWs, Jensen Interceptors, Ferraris, Lamborghinis, and, overwhelmingly, countless "Porches."

We found ourselves standing in the middle of a gigantic resting place for once-splendid sports and luxury cars, the vast majority of which were of European origin. It was a morbid and spellbinding sight. A few of the wrecks still held clues as to their life stories; others had been looted far too extensively. Here in L.A., cars still did rust,

just not quite as rapidly as elsewhere—it "never" rains in California, after all—and the only moisture was that coming from our eyes as we toured this most exclusive of scrapyards, courtesy of Rudi Klein.

With high walls shielding the junkyard from inquisitive eyes, it seemed as if this was where the true ghosts of automobile history roamed. There they lay, burnt out, twisted, half hidden, sliced in half, incomplete or partly cannibalized, side by side or on top of one another—cars that in their day had been not just the most prized possessions of their owners but also the flagship models of their manufacturers. While we were there we would of course have liked to ask Klein about the origins of this or that car, or to bombard him with penetrating questions, but to do so would have carried too great a risk of alienating the former butcher. So we kept our mouths firmly shut, stunned at what we were seeing.

Intoxicated by the intensity of what was in front of us, we strolled among all these treasures, little realizing that in seventeen years' time they would be worth twice, three times, or even many more multiples of their price. For values simply exploded over that space of time. Who then could have the slightest inkling that well-heeled citizens of our planet would have been willing to pay almost $300,000 for a semi decrepit Bugatti dredged up from Lago Maggiore? Or nearly $2 million for a 1956 Frua-bodied Maserati A6G/2000 from the just-discovered Baillon collection—a car that looked as if had been pelted with rocks from a great height? Or even nearly $20 million for a dust-covered forty-year-old Ferrari that Alain Delon had owned for scarcely a year and was found in the same collection? If anyone was to have the right nose to sniff out this kind of thing, it was that modest German in the middle of a surreal junkyard on American soil.

Klein, however, never intended to build up a "collection" in the normal sense of the word—he simply stockpiled stuff that other people were throwing out. Time was when Klein, as a butcher from Rüsselsheim, near Frankfurt, used to deliver sausages in the

exclusive Hamburg suburb of Blankenese, in particular to Count Luckner and the Reemstma family; however, by the age of twenty-five, his wanderlust had drawn him to Canada. There he worked as a butcher in a supermarket before moving to the United States. And it was in the US that he bought his first crashed car, a Mercedes 300SL; pretty soon he was acquiring further accident-damaged German cars, secured from insurance companies or auctions—for a song.

In 1971, he and a friend opened a breaker's yard. Time and time again he would pick up cars for the price of a cup of coffee, and this is how he came by Burt Lancaster's 280-series Mercedes, a Rolls-Royce convertible that belonged to Tony Curtis, and Sonny

and Cher's Ferrari 250 LM. And neglected prewar cars, often brought over from Europe to the States by high-ranking American military personnel, tended to be ignored—except by Rudi Klein.

It was in 1974, during the time of the first oil crisis, that Klein was able to secure large volumes of expensive cars in all kinds of condition, predominantly Porsches and Mercedes. "No one wanted those cars at that point," he said. As soon as the oil crisis had passed, Klein was able to resell these treasures at a hefty profit. Take the Mercedes 300 SL alone: he succeeded in collecting twenty examples of this legendary model in the United States, shipping them back to Germany for resale. But it was in the 1980s, when the great classic-car boom began to take hold, that Klein would hit the big time.

CRUMPLED LUXURY
Welcome to L.A.: At first glance the eye can take in no more than a tiny fraction of this vast luxury-car empire.

Having heard talk of Klein's unique still-life collection, automobile restorers from every corner of the world laid siege to his site and paid stupendous prices to be able to extract even more money from classic-car aficionados back home. In parallel, Klein would rent out or sell cars such as Porsche 928s or Mercedes 600s to film companies, but the moviemakers were more interested in pleasing their audiences by blowing that precious scrap metal to smithereens on the cinema screen or exploiting the cars some other way.

Klein was in the right place at just the right time. "The movie business is long since gone," he told us when we were there. "Nowadays they do it all on computers." Fortunately, his old cars remained just as highly prized by collectors as they had always been, even though by the turn of the millennium Klein was making most of his money from modern insurance write-offs.

Yet he burned cash, too—though clearly not by design. As an example, he put close to eight million Marks into a project by one-time racer and self-styled automaker Erich Bitter. Klein believed in

Bitter's vision that with enough cash behind him he could turn Opel models into high-end luxury cars; Klein pumped in million after million into this risky venture—and lost. At the end of the day he was in any case able to recover the money thanks to the often-excessive prices he charged for the various items sold in his scrapyard.

Just to set foot on the driveway next to the junkyard office was enough to stir up a morbid sense of fascination with disaster: around sixty of Klein's two hundred crumpled Porsche 365s were stacked on three stories of metal racking; Cabrios, Speedsters, and Coupés were all on display at the same time there. As a showcase of high-end scrap, it was both mesmerizing and macabre, as much for its quality as for its sheer quantity: some 5,000 one-time dream cars had been laid to rest on the 16,000-square-meter site, dominated by a total of 2,000 Porsches and 1,500 Mercedes.

And the list went on: a Rolls-Royce Silver Shadow II perched on top of a Maserati, and alongside it some greenery pushing its way up through a 1952 "Adenauer" Mercedes 300 automatic, complete with its original Becker radio. Glancing around, it was easy to spot a Dino Ferrari, a Mercedes 220 Coupé, a Maserati-engined Citroën SM, an Aston Martin Vantage, a Mark II Jaguar, and a pair of 1950s Packards—all open to the skies.

And then there was a completely derelict Chevrolet Corvair Cabrio. After we'd plucked up courage to ask Klein what it might be worth, his answer of $7,500 quickly knocked any crazy notions out of our heads. Clearly, if you were lucky enough to find something for $50,000 somewhere else, you might be charged $75,000 for the same item at Klein's if he did not like the look of your face. For one of the legendary Fuhrmann Porsche engines Klein might ask double the going rate. And sometimes he refused to sell components off cars that were already two-thirds stripped: those customers, who must have for some reason fallen out of favor with him, were left with a stark choice—either take the complete wreck for an obscene price or go home empty handed.

HEAD OF STATE
Rudi Klein as he liked to see himself: lord and master of the luxurious trappings discarded by the rich and famous.

The greatest treasures of all proved to be those hidden away in a series of huts and barns scattered over the site and in the surrounding area, too. In a gloomy corridor lurked a Bristol, a Rolls-Royce Silver Wraith II, a Stutz IV-Porte, and two Bentleys. In other barns, countless generations of birds had for decades been depositing their droppings on open-topped (Mercedes) Pagodas as well as a range of Mercedes sedans from the hippie era.

In another corner, pressed tight against the wall, languished an extremely rare BMW coupe—so rare, in fact, that we did not know what it was. We sent a picture to BMW in Munich straight away. Word came back that it was a BMW 502 and that it was one of just two examples rebodied with coachwork by Autenrieth in Darmstadt as the "Marburg" or "Nürnberg." Both of these rarities were currently believed lost. BMW did in fact consider buying the car back and went as far as to inquire. Klein's immediate response was that he was not interested in selling.

Yet neither did he have any interest in restoring these vehicles himself. "I much prefer them in their original state," he snapped. Misshapen and twisted but not tinkered with—that's how he liked the car bodies to be. Lost in thought despite our presence, he strolled off towards his gigantic rack of engines; here he gave an affectionate pat to the original Porsche engine out of a 1951 1300 and pointed towards the rear end of a rare 356 Carrera Coupé built in 1964. The car still housed its so-called "Königswellenmotor" or vertical shaft engine. Complete with dual ignition, it was developed by former Porsche chief Dr. Ernst Fuhrmann and produced 130 horsepower. Klein was also clearly proud of the very first 911 S Targa, built in 1967, which he conceded he might, in exceptional circumstances, want to restore—or maybe not.

And at that point, entirely out of character with his shy, introverted demeanor, he suddenly insisted on showing us something—the holy of holies of all his dust-covered treasures. We drove to a half-collapsed mattress warehouse close by, and when we got there we could hardly believe what we saw: densely packed alongside one another in the huge, dark warehouse, and draped with makeshift tattered cotton sheeting, sat a collection of crash-damaged cars that turned our legs to jelly the instant we clapped eyes on them. One was the Mercedes 600 formerly belonging to Playboy boss Hugh Hefner, and next to it a 1950s Mercedes 300 Coupé, a one-off with coachwork by Baur.

In addition, there was a Spohn-bodied Maybach SW38 full cabriolet, whose top hung limply down in tatters; also two Iso Grifos—a coupe and a cabrio—apropos of which Klein let slip he still harbored the desire to do the Ennstal-Classic at some time in the open sports one. On and on it went: a Lamborghini Miura, a Bora and a Mexico from Maserati, a Cadillac Eldorado convertible, an Aston Martin DB6, a 1957 BMW 503 cabrio, a Ferrari without its nose, a Mercedes 300 Cabriolet with German plates, and and and . . .

It is said that a few bounty hunters from well-known German automakers had been seen standing there open-mouthed as they tried to persuade Klein to part with the particular prizes they were tracking down. Consider the Mercedes 300 SL Gullwing with all-aluminum bodywork: according to Daimler, just twenty-nine examples were built. Klein's response at the time would invariably have been a straight no—or he might have named a clearly prohibitive price for the Stuttgart sports car.

Even Ritchie Klein, the casino mega-mogul (unrelated to Rudi Klein), became acquainted with our friend from Rüsselsheim. The reason, explained the hotel-chain owner, was that he had an original Adolf Hitler Mercedes in his museum in one of his hotels, and he therefore wanted Rudi Klein's Horch 855 Spezial Roadster to place alongside it; Rudi had insisted that the Horch was the car used by Eva Braun, Hitler's lover and, for just a few days, his wife. On several occasions Ritchie had placed a blank check on the table, urging Rudi to fill in whatever amount he wanted for the Horch, the sole

DECLINE AND FALL
Welcome to a world of rust, battered bodywork,
and shattered dreams: one of around two
hundred Porsche 356s in the giant junkyard.

survivor of only seven examples built. And each time, Rudi sent the billionaire back home empty handed.

"It was only 'that man [Ferdinand] Piëch' who got anything from me," Rudi Klein told us, "because Piëch is the only person who understands anything about cars and automotive technology." In actual fact, in addition to a Horch 780, "that man Piëch" came away with the purported Eva Braun Horch—on loan. The two cars took up their new residence in the Audi Museum straight away.

Both Horchs are still there, the 780 unrestored in the reserve collection and the 855 fully restored in the main exhibition area. But perhaps not for much longer. Klein, true to type, had pushed for a deal that allowed Audi to keep or exhibit the cars for twenty years—on the condition that the German marque undertook, at the very least, a full restoration of the Spezial Roadster. Audi said yes. That's what anyone would call a win-win, at least for as long as the contract runs.

For in 2018 Klein's sons, Justin and Benji, had been due to get the cars back again, and it looked like those cars would be worth many multiples of their earlier value. Yet Audi Tradition is still unable to confirm that Klein's 855 Spezial Roadster is actually Eva Braun's; nevertheless, the model remains one of the most important cars in the Audi Museum collection. "We're already shedding a few tears" at the prospect of soon having to send the 855 back to an uncertain fate in L.A., conceded Thomas Frank, head of Audi Tradition, in 2017. That is why there are moves afoot to extend the deal.

Yet the most magnificent of all Klein's treasures has remained completely off limits, even for Volkswagen CEO Ferdinand Piëch: the personal car driven by the legendary prewar Mercedes works racing driver Rudolf Caracciola, a Mercedes 500 K Spezial Coupé built in 1935. Klein bought it from the Cars of the Stars museum, and after he had had it restored it was shown at Pebble Beach in 1978. "It was originally a convertible but was involved in an accident and then rebuilt as a coupé," Klein told us, barely managing to conceal his great pride. "Caracciola still carried on driving the car himself, though." In 1980, Klein brought this gem of a car along to a Mercedes show, but legend has it that the car failed to start the event. Klein is said to have been so furious with the car that he packed it back onto its trailer, shipped it back home, and banished it to a dark and dingy hut. It is believed that he never touched the car again.

When we saw the car, complete with its 160-horsepower supercharged engine, it looked absolutely ready for the road—apart from its four flat tires. In late 2019, Mercedes confirmed that it still had not acquired the car, and it is assumed that this unique specimen is—just like before—still waiting in a backyard lockup somewhere in the L.A. area. Or something like that.

The same probably holds true for those other by-catch vehicles that Klein scooped up on his fishing expeditions—models that were once the dream cars of the middle classes. A Volvo 1800S, a Maserati Biturbo, a DKW Munga, and an Alfa Romeo Montreal; a phalanx of Porsche 914s, a Chevrolet Corvette and a Nash Ambassador—all sitting under the bleaching sun, day in and day out. He spoke of other cars in other places, too, and mentioned a recently acquired Chrysler Airflow located in Ohio:

"You should go and have a look at it!" Maybe he wanted to sell it? Heaven forbid . . .

But who would actually get something from his near-inexhaustible stockpile? Worried about rummagers, he never allowed just anyone onto the site—the risk of people stealing stuff was much too great, he insisted. The danger of people getting on his nerves was no less a worry. "I never sell individual spare parts at all," he continued. "But if someone wants to put together a whole car or several cars, he can get them from me complete with engine, transmission, and bodywork."

But only if the price is right . . .

LAST EXIT FLORENCE,
SOUTH CENTRAL LOS ANGELES

SCRAP CITY
At first glance it looks like no more than a giant heap of buckled metal and rust. Look closer and you'll find automotive gems everywhere—alongside, above, below, and even jammed inside one another.

AN ALLEY OF PORSCHES
Just inside the main entrance, the site's precious few visitors are greeted by a long wall stacked with Porsche 356s.

IF LIGHTS COULD SPEAK . . .
Whether they're from a young(ish) BMW or an old Benz, these headlights stare out sadly from their sockets. ▲

STACKABLE SEDANS
They are stored wherever space can be found. There's no clear system of where the wrecks end up on the pile. Only the real gems are brought into the barns and warehouses.

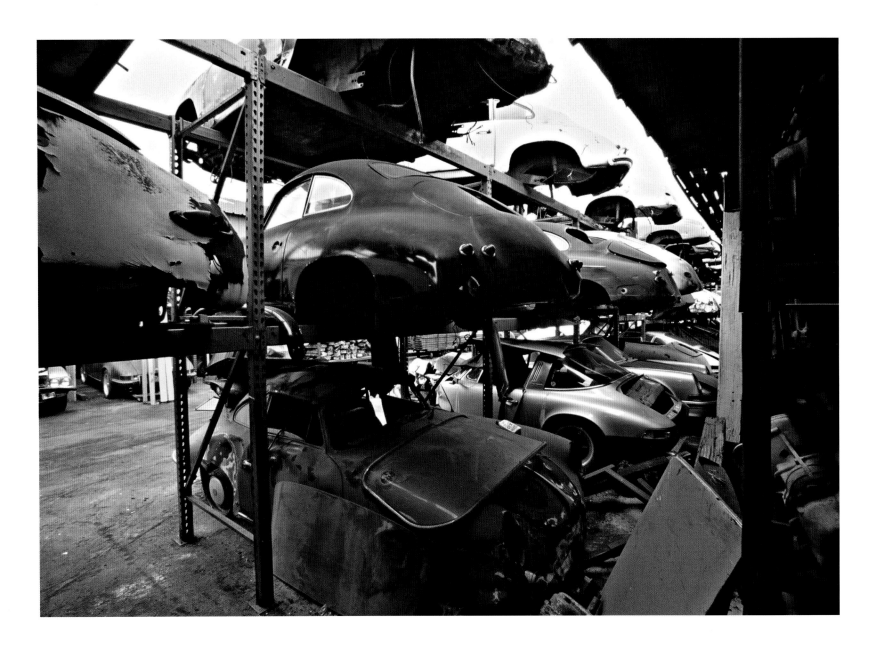

REAR ASPECT
Body shells by the dozen: Americans always
had a special soft spot for the Porsche 356,
and they left the remains with Rudi Klein when
they finished.

A QUESTION OF DETAIL
There's no halting the onward march of
automotive decay, but there are always details
that betray a car's identity—as in the case of this
blue Nash Ambassador Custom.

CRASHED OUT
This Porsche 911 Targa had just 19,000 miles on the clock when an accident forced its untimely demise. Klein's compound also houses what is claimed to be the first-ever 911 S Targa off the line.

RANDOM SELECTION
Component parts from stripped vehicles are
rarely sorted and by no means always kept under
cover—even rare and highly sought-after items
are hard to find among the mountain of parts. ◄

WEST COAST BLUES
The saying goes that it never rains in California—
but even high-end bodywork suffers when
abandoned under open skies. ▲

PORSCHE PARADISE
Anyone after Porsche spares will always strike
luck at Klein's yard—as long as they're prepared
to pay quite a price. As for 356s, there are some
two hundred here, in all stages of decay.

DOUBLE WHAMMY
The 911 on top had suffered a frontal impact when it was brought into Porche Foreign Auto Dismantling, while the Bentley was burnt out.

Long-since-forgotten dramas have left their mark in bizarre forms: the Jaguar E-Type nose section is unmistakable, but nothing else remains of this once-splendid Brit.

BRIT POP
It's as if this Bentley simply wanted to pull over and park: even the famous radiator mascot and fog lights are still in place.

FORCE OF NATURE
Plants aren't fussy about whether it is plain sheet metal or something more special; the grass will grow wherever there's a gap in the ground.

PLANT POT
Even in this once-dingy suburb of Los Angeles, nature will find a way of consuming old car bodies. ◣

ON THE TERRACES
The only place you'll find interesting architecture in the junkyard is inside the vehicles—this is the dashboard of a Volvo P1800S. ◤

A KIND OF BLUE
The upholstery colors in this Nash interior put up a brave fight against sunlight and decay. Also on the site were a Chevrolet Corvair and Corvette, a Nash Ambassador, and a pair of Packards.

BLACK AND WHITE
Sometimes it doesn't matter what the model is—
when all the colors have faded, the details take
on their own aesthetic.

SWAN SONG
This 1950s Packard's elegant hood mascot seems to be giving one final bow to its audience of assembled scrap. ◄

BREAKING THE LIGHT
The crazy patterns in this old Porsche 911's smashed side window produce a magical effect in the light. ▲

RUSTY RETREAT
Aristocratic automobiles enjoy nothing better than the undisturbed outdoors for their declining years. This Bentley has rusted to take on a uniform iron-oxide look like a Calder sculpture.

WILD WHEELS
Wildflowers have pushed their way up through this old wire-spoke wheel to obscure it from view. It no longer seems to belong to any of the cars. ◣

RECOVERED WRECK?
You could picture this Mercedes 220 Cabriolet being dredged up from the bottom of a lagoon. ◥

INSTRUMENTS ON DISPLAY
This highly aristocratic Bristol is typically British, with its right-hand drive, wooden dashboard, and impressive array of instruments. To the right are the controls for the preselector transmission.

No more cooling: the only temperature changes
taking place on this old Mercedes are due to the
highs and lows of the merciless sun.

SECRET POWER
In earlier times, Rolls-Royce refused to disclose
performance figures, stating only that engine
power was "sufficient."

COLLAGE OF CARS
Jensen, Porsche, Mercedes: this crazy combination of machinery is not so much a scrapheap as an enormous work of art for morbidly inclined car enthusiasts.

German cars are in the majority here: in addition
to Porsches, the observant visitor will spot
a couple of BMWs, such as this 2002, and of
course large numbers of Mercedes of every era.

THE PLAY OF NATURE
The rear of this 1955 Packard Patrician is slowly
disappearing into the undergrowth. Rudi Klein
was never too interested in American cars.

This prewar Mercedes 170 S still has its vacuum-tube radio receiver—it's easy to imagine it tuning in to German propaganda stations.

PUSHED TO THE EXTREME
Even the outer limits of the site are stacked skyward with high-end scrap—topped, naturally, by a Porsche 356.

WHERE EXOTICS MEET
Glamour amid the grime: an Alfa Romeo Montreal, complete with slatted eyelids, sits on top of a Zagato-bodied Maserati Biturbo and the rear end of a Porsche 944. ◣

BEYOND SALVATION
This Mercedes 220 from the 1950s has been completely gutted; the Porsche 911 perched on its roof still wears its ADAC emblem, rare in the United States. ▶

AVANT GARDE
Its capricious Maserati engine gave the individualistic Citroën SM a reputation for trouble, but in terms of design it has still not found an equal. This example was imported from France.

SHAPE OF THE CENTURY
Porsche 911s heaped up like a bargain basement
sale. Today's high prices mean that even badly
damaged examples are seen as suitable cases
for restoration.

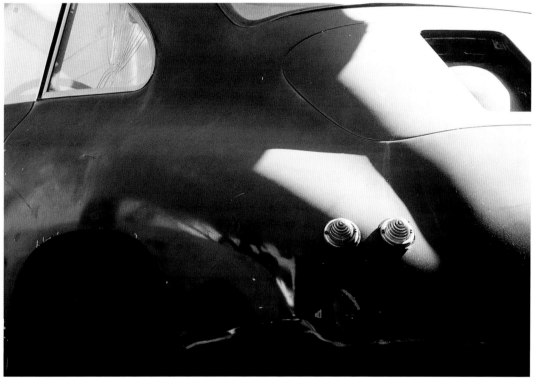

SENSE OF STYLE
Today's enthusiasts are prepared to pay big
money for Fuchs-type wheels, as on the Porsche
911 above; the 356 has endless variations, many
of them present on Klein's site. The rear lights
alone set collectors' pulses racing, whether they
are the teardrop type or bullet shaped.

This weighty V-8 once powered a Rolls-Royce, but its owner probably never set eyes on it—for that, he employed a chauffeur.

CROWN OF STARS
This Mercedes looks as if it has expired of
old age; someone has ripped out its innards
and put them on the roof to form a weather-
beaten crown.

REAR VIEW
The truncated back end of a Mercedes 190 SL is part of the all-encompassing still-life picture at the Los Angeles site.

STAMP OF QUALITY
Still just legible on the chassis plate are the words "Daimler-Benz Aktiengesellschaft, Werk Untertürkheim" and, less clearly, the model year of this 220 series: 1952.

BEACH BOY
A surfer's favorite: a first-generation T1 VW bus
finds itself washed up in Klein's junkyard.

69

COVER SHEET
Someone years ago appears to have put a protective sheet over this highly collectible Mercedes 300 SEL 6.3—but the car has been forgotten anyway. ◀

SCREENS OUT, DUST IN
Windows left open have allowed decades of dust to blow into vehicle interiors—even when they are stored in the barns. "Patina" is a major understatement. ▲

71

A NOSE IN FRONT
In their heyday, these two rounded noses would have been pushing to the front of the line in every passing lane.

Klein's junkyard might be the world's most peculiar auto museum, but it houses real rarities, such as this Mercedes 300 Coupé, a one-off made in the 1950s by Stuttgart specialist coachbuilder Baur.

BRONZE AGE

It's hard to believe, but there were people who used to come to this scrapyard to find spare parts for their Rolls-Royces.

RUST SCARS
Where the paint has peeled away, oxidization
has turned vehicles into surreal compositions.

A BULL ON A SKATEBOARD
Few traces of its spectacular Verde Metallizzata paint still cling to this Lamborghini Miura's bodywork—and it can only be shifted with the aid of a wagon underneath. The Jensen Interceptor in Metallic Acqua Blue does not appear to be much more mobile.

Bird droppings are the worst possible news for automotive paintwork. Pigeons and other birds fly in and out of Klein's barns at will, adding an even more corrosive element to the blanket covering of dust and dirt. ◀

Even BMW is uncertain whether this coupe (lower picture) is the Marburg or Nürnberg: both were one-offs made by coachbuilder Autenrieth in the 1950s, based on the chassis of the 502. Back then there was also a convertible companion, by the name of Hannover. ▲

TEST DRIVE, SIR?
The Autenrieth BMW looks ready to go for a quick spin—apart from the pigeon patina and the Mercedes blocking its path.

We don't yet know whether this Mercedes 300 SL will come to be restored at company headquarters or where it will finally end up. Today, prices for an example with this extent of corrosion run to $330,000 or more. In the background sits a Ferrari Dino 308.

POINTS DEDUCTED
This Porsche 356 has been fitted with an
aftermarket tuner's engine cover, which would
have to be replaced for any concours restoration
project. Suitable parts are close to hand at
Klein's junkyard.

ECONOMIC MIRACLE

To drive a Mercedes 300 S Cabriolet in the 1950s was a sign that you'd made it big. Very few were built, and Klein's example even has a pennant on the left fender.

ARISTOCRATIC ENGINE
A genuine engineering jewel, and a very valuable one, too: the 1964 Porsche 356 C Carrera in Klein's yard features the remarkable "Königswellen" engine designed by Dr. Ernst Fuhrmann, giving 130 horsepower thanks to its dual ignition.

ALUMINIUM—PRECIOUS METAL
One of the very special Gullwings: this 300 SL may have a covering of bird droppings, but it is complete with engine and transmission. What's extra special is that everything is made of aluminum; only twenty-one of these lightweight coupes were ever made.

WELL PRESERVED
All bases covered: hidden in its shadowy barn, this prewar Mercedes has not seen the light of day for ages. Perhaps that has helped it stay in good shape—right down to the tires.

BAVARIAN BEAUTY
A rarity on eight wheels: mounted on a wagon, this BMW 503 Cabriolet (lower picture) dates back to 1957. Between May 1956 and March 1959, BMW produced just 139 examples. ▼

SHADOW WORLD
These icons of automotive history have at least been kept dry over the years: a Maybach Cabrio-Limousine (center) and Rudolf Caracciola's Mercedes 500 K (center right). ▲

HIGHWAY CRUISER
Parked among the multitude of Mercedes
sedans is this piece of true Americana—a Lincoln
Continental coupe, model year 1967.

THE ITALIAN AMERICAN
The Iso Grifo is one of Giugiaro's earliest
masterpieces. Under their hoods, the cars
concealed potent Chevrolet or Ford V-8s with
capacities ranging from 5.4 to 7 liters.

PATINA OF MANY AGES
Blissfully ignorant of the value of the many dream cars below them, generations of pigeons have scattered their droppings indiscriminately across every treasure.

PAN-ALPINE CASTOFFS
Side by side in dirt and dust, high-end cars from Germany and Italy—a Porsche 911 2.4, a Mercedes 220 S from the 1950s, and a Maserati Mistral raised on axle stands.

TUNNEL VISION
Every last square inch of Klein's site is crammed
full. Among the cars jammed in the narrow
passageway are a weirdly retro Stutz IV Porte,
with the roof of a Rolls-Royce visible behind.

TOTAL GRIDLOCK
This crazy jam is like something out of a Jacques Tati movie—Rudi Klein's treasures seem to have been placed anywhere and everywhere in his barns.

COMPANY CAR—WITH A DIFFERENCE
Mercedes officials are very interested in this one:
the Stuttgart automaker specially converted the
500 K Special Coupé as a high-performance
road car for its works race driver Rudolf
Caracciola in 1935.

SOVEREIGN SYMBOL
The Mercedes star has weathered the external elements with its dignity intact. ▶

AUDI'S DIFFERENT
This Audi 80 was still covered by its ten-year rust warranty when we visited years ago—but it has problems of a completely different sort. ▲

DUST TRAPS
Each of the barns houses a different set of priceless treasures—such as this Maserati Mexico behind two Porsche 911s, all of them under a thick layer of dust.

PRICE PARITY
In their day, each of these cars would have cost the price of a large house: two Mercedes SL Roadsters with hardtops and an aluminum gullwing, framed by a red Maserati Merak and a BMW 503 Cabriolet.

BUNNY BOSS'S BENZ
Once the absolute last word in luxury but now somewhat battered, the Mercedes 600 under the blue tarp was once owned by Playboy founder Hugh Hefner.

CRYING CABLE TEARS
It's not quite Marvin, the depressed and neglected robot from *The Hitchhiker's Guide to the Galaxy* who wept tears of wire—but the butchered BMW 2000 CS does give the impression of a mechanical skull.

BROKEN BOXER
Rudi Klein could not remember how this BMW motorcycle engine came to be on his site—and he didn't seem to care.

TRIDENT
The second of just 482 built: Klein hoarded at least one pair of Maserati Mexicos. Today, these classy grand turismos are practically worth their weight in gold.

THE DARKEST CORNER
Scarcely any light ever penetrates into the deepest recesses of Klein's barns and huts, but even there, in the gloom, stripped-out luxury cars like this Rolls-Royce are to be found.

INTERIOR INSIGHTS
The questions that have been asked a hundred
times: Who used to sit in this driving seat?
What went on in their dream car? If only wrecks
could talk . . .

A WHIFF OF BOND
In the movie *The Living Daylights*, James Bond drives an Aston Martin V8—and here in this hall, this example was laid to rest.

PERSONAL FAVORITE
This very pretty 1964 Iso Grifo A3/L Spyder
has an American V-8 engine. It was one of Rudi
Klein's all-time favorites, and he hoped one day
to rebuild it and take part in a classic-car rally
in Bavaria.

NO GADGETS STANDARD
It might look like James Bond's company car after losing a race against Goldfinger—but this is a DB6, and it was an Aston Martin DB5 that Sean Connery drove on those two occasions.

FRONTAL SANDWICH
Half a Bentley topped with a slice of Porsche.
The German émigré is an extremely careful
scrapyard owner and cannot bear to throw
anything away.

CRUMPLE ZONE
The obstacle that this Porsche 356 crashed into must have been pretty substantial. The car is a typical candidate for Klein's high-end junkyard.

FLYING BLIND
Clean the screen and drive off? This splendid
1949 Packard makes that seem perfectly
possible. And who remembers the "Avus"
steering-wheel rim cover that every second
Beetle used to possess?

THE STEP-PORSCHE
Even VW-Porsche 914s are worth buying,
thought Rudi Klein. That contrasts with Germany,
where the fan base has yet to give the models
serious recognition.

WORM'S-EYE VIEW
Decay made beautiful: it will never make it back onto the road, but the way this Porsche 356 has turned green has its own melancholy charm.

LOOP THE LOOP
The Targa rollover hoop may well have protected the driver of this heavily crumpled Porsche, but the life of the car itself is over. ▲

LONG-DISTANCE RUNNER
With its interior caked in dust, this Mercedes sedan looks as if it has returned from thirty years in the desert. Its odometer reads just 32,000 miles—but it's only the older sort with just five digits. ▶

THREE SHADES OF GRAY
This car's original owner must have been thrilled with the model's classy two-tone color scheme. The stylish dark red was only added later as the steel panels began to corrode in the open air.

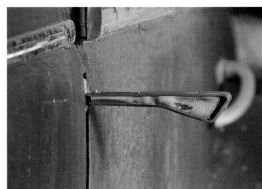

DIRECTION INDICATOR
Most definitely dead: the small warning-lights panel and the headlights on this abandoned Maserati and the jammed semaphore arm on the Mercedes—don't bother heeding their indications.

Wash me, please, it's springtime . . . This
Volvo 1800 S, a model that was for a while
manufactured by Jensen in Britain, looks in
good enough shape for a quick spin around
the block. ◀

All we know is that this car is a convertible, has
a very thin steering-wheel rim, and could date
from the 1960s. Some cars in Klein's compound
have been stripped so completely bare that it is
impossible still to identify them. ▲

SPORTING SPIRIT
A speedometer reading up to 250 kilometers per hour—in its time, that was top-level sports-car performance. The owner of this Maserati must have appreciated its impressive instrument display—until something brought the whole car to a permanent halt.

ORGAN DONORS
This "economic miracle" Mercedes, with its prewar shape, has not yet been completely stripped bare; it is surrounded by heaps of spare parts—engines, ignition coils, connecting rods, and other valuable items. This paradise for treasure hunters measures 16,000 square meters.

People, weather, and the passage of time. These
three factors are still the most potent aging
influences—yet still visible are design details over
which the cars' creators sweated blood all those
years ago.

BOURGEOIS PRIDE
A 2.8-liter straight six, 160 horsepower, and a sleek coupe shape: everything that once distinguished this Mercedes 280 C and made its owner proud, now reduced to a tangle of twisted metal.

MERCEDES RESTING PLACE
Even today, the Mercedes models of the 1960s still seem like dream cars. Impressive is the red coupe with its lightly pockmarked roof; behind it is the flagship sedan of its day, the 300 SEL 6.3.

FANTASY FORM

Stretching skywards in the sun like an alien with gaping jaws, the battered rear end of this Porsche 356 looks more like a work of art than a source of spare parts.

CHROME—NOT JUNK
When Rolls-Royce chromed its components, they were designed to last forever. This grille proves the British held good on that promise.

BURNT OFFERINGS
All these cars are so burnt out that nothing can
be done with them anymore. Even so, Rudi Klein
still coveted them.

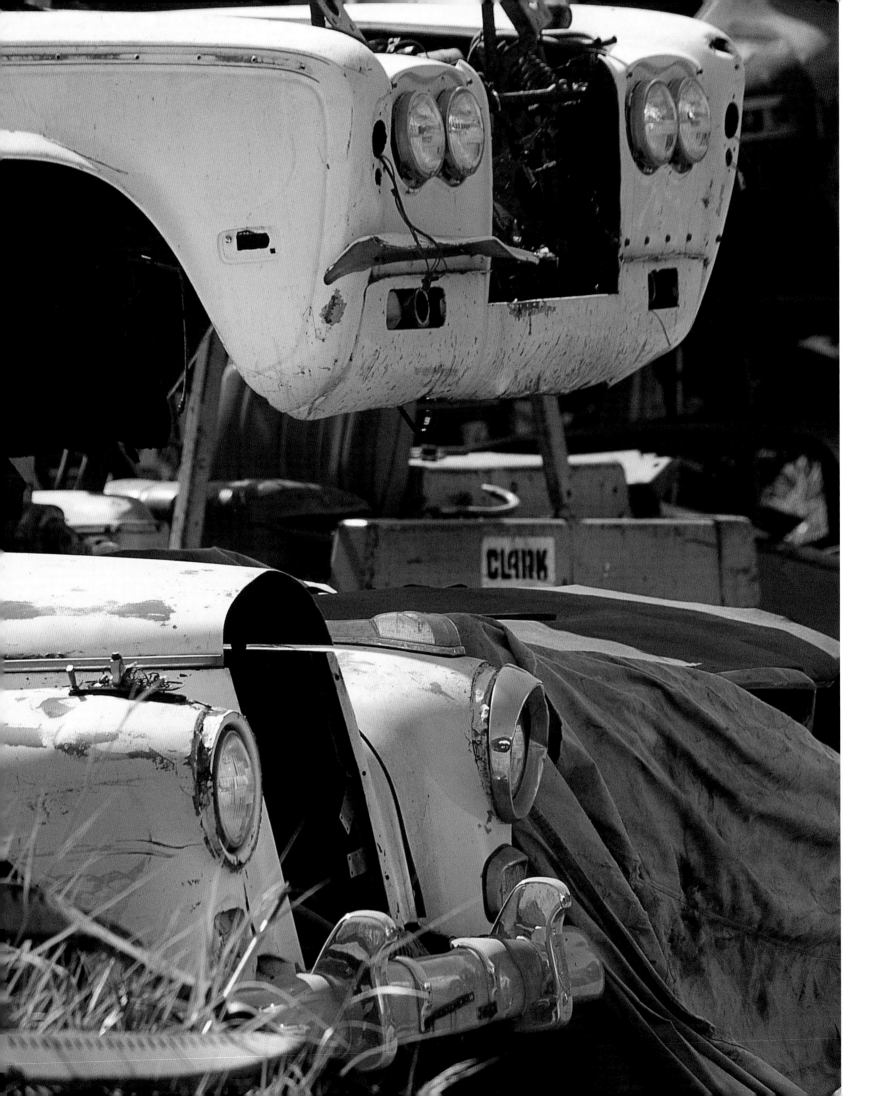

MISSING GRILLES
Rolls-Royce and Mercedes—each has at some time or other been debated as the builder of the best car in the world. But here two of those acknowledged luxury greats rest peacefully on top of one another as the rust takes hold. ◄

LET THE SUNSHINE IN
Hardtop or traditional fabric convertible roof? The textiles are the first to rot away, but a few years later the metal roofs also begin their transformation into brown dust. ▲

PONTOONS TOGETHER
The Mercedes-Benz 219 series featured six-cylinder engines and dominated the upper-middle-class market. Today, this entitles them to keep company with the high-end models in the scrapyard.

THE PEOPLE'S PORSCHE
The Porsche 914 had an air-cooled flat-four engine and was built in conjunction with Volkswagen. Around 120,000 "Volks-Porsches" were made, with around 70 percent exported to the United States.

KEY TO THE HIGHWAY
White steering wheel, column shift, original radio, full interior equipment—and even the key in the ignition. Today, something like this "Adenauer" Mercedes 300 would be the perfect starting point for a restoration.

MEDIUM RED—PROBABLY
The paintwork here might have been a medium red, perhaps even metallic. After a while it doesn't matter anyway, as this Mercedes 280SE Coupé will one day morph to rust red all over.

FULL-SIZE BARGE
With its distinctive twin stacked headlights, this
Pontiac Bonneville peers out cheekily from amid
the scrap. It is one of the few American cars in
Klein's curious collection.

AIR AND GRACES
These elegant Campagnolo alloy wheels, complete with their central knock-off hub fixings, carry the standard-fit Pirelli tires—and there's actually still air in them.

ITALY, CALIFORNIA STYLE
This Ferrari 330 GTC California has had almost every one of its parts stripped off—except for the unmistakable prancing-horse Ferrari badge that still adorns its nose.

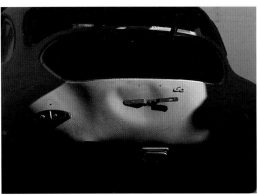

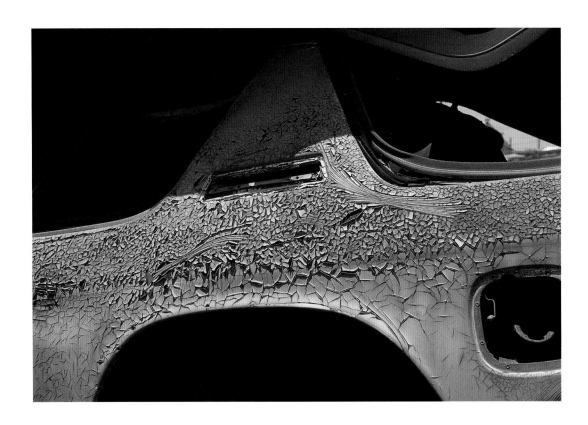

PAINTING GAMES
Paint isn't always simply paint: sometimes it
weathers strangely, dries out, or peels away;
other paint stays as shiny as on the day the car
left the showroom. That's the luck of the draw . . .

In its day, a Mercedes 220 S Coupé like this would have been out of reach for the majority of people—but now, this worn-out example is on display, warts and all.

KNOCKS AND DINGS
Many of them stacked three stories high, these wrecks that once showed only minor parking dings are now subject to much greater indignities.

MORE CRUMPLE ZONES
You just have to hope that the people traveling in these cars when they crashed were able to escape unscathed from the twisted wreckage.

BACK TO NATURE
With the growth of each stem, this Bentley S3 returns ever closer to nature—enthusiasts will need courage, as fewer than 1,300 examples were built between 1962 and 1965.

RUSTY COMPOST
Front axles are casually scattered among the undergrowth, and the shock-absorber rods look just as eager to sting as the spikes on the cacti in the background.

MAKING AN IMPRESSION
As nighttime drew closer, we had to take our leave of these treasured specimens. To this day, those powerful impressions remain with us.

THE SUN SETS
Just one last picture, and then it is goodbye
forever. As the last of the daylight fades away,
it is time for those parting shots. Never before
and never since would this California classic-car
junkyard allow photographic access like this.

MAMMOTH TASK
Dieter Rebmann stands dwarfed by his mountainous assignment: "If you stumble across an old Rolls-Royce in a scrapyard somewhere, you'll photograph it because it's such a rare find. But here in California there was an excess of everything—I was faced with ten thousand potential subjects, and I didn't know where to begin . . ."

Dieter Rebmann was born in Sindelfingen, near Stuttgart, Germany, in 1955 and began his working life in marketing. After seven years in business he decided to devote himself exclusively to photography. He became a trainee with Paul Swiridoff, one of the major figures in the profession at that time, who had become well known for a very individualistic style that showed people in a fresh light.

Swiridoff's photographic work included exceptional portraits of exceptional personalities from academia, politics, and business in Germany. His advice to Rebmann as trainee was to "learn to see the light"—and from that point on, this served as the guiding principle in Rebmann's work.

After completing his training, he honed his style with assignments for photographers based in New York, Virginia, and Florida. He also had the opportunity to look over the shoulder of Vince Finnegan in the latter's capacity as official White House photographer.

In 1983, he completed his master's degree at the Bavarian State School of Photography. As a freelancer, he opted for new challenges in the shape of work in René Staud's Hi-Tech Studios in Stuttgart.

Since 1992, Rebmann has chosen to concentrate on automotive photography, his specialty being "the subject in harmony with its surroundings." In addition to his work for well-known automotive manufacturers, he maintains a strong interest in two- and four-wheeled classics. The year 1998 saw the publication of his lavish two-volume collection *Ride Free Forever: The Legend of Harley-Davidson*, and for many years he has been providing images for large-format calendars on themes such as Porsche 911, Vespa, BMW motorcycles, superbikes, and Harley-Davidson.

With the arrival of digital photography, Rebmann made it clear that what was important was how old and new techniques were combined. He was keen to safeguard traditional photography and to understand it as craftsmanship yet, at the same time, also to transform it creatively and to employ the latest image processing technology. His maxim is this: "You can always take a poor picture and make a better one out of it, but it is much more sensible to start with a good picture and turn it into an even better one—or even one that's perfect." After all, art also relies on skilled craftsmanship.

The photographs in this book have all been produced with purely analog techniques.

Further information is available at www.dieter-rebmann.de.

AUTOMOTIVE PHOTOGRAPHER
In addition to his commercial work for the automotive industry and motoring magazines, Dieter Rebmann is also a highly regarded photographic artist.

His outlets include *Die Welt*, *Playboy*, *ramp*, and a range of classic magazines, as well as newspapers and other publications in Switzerland. He also contributes to various customer publications. His current book projects include the history of automobiles, car models, and adventures. And also junkyards . . .

Find out more at www.rolandloewisch.de.

Roland Löwisch, model year 1959, was drawn to journalism while studying business administration and began his career as a local reporter in the Hamburg, Germany, area. Upon graduation, he was able to combine his profession with his passion for cars when he joined *Auto Bild* magazine. That led him to *STERN* and then back to *Auto Bild*, this time as chief reporter. He also assumed the editorship of the prestigious publication *Auto Forum*. Later, he would become editor in chief of *Auto Bild Sportscars*.

Since 2006, Löwisch has worked as a freelance writer specializing in high-end cars, sports cars, off-roaders, and classic vehicles. This broad spectrum of work means that Löwisch spends more than one-third of each year traveling internationally.

AUTOMOTIVE EDITOR
Roland Löwisch feels very much at home in the world of classic vehicles—even though he spends about half his working week driving modern premium and sports cars.

IN MEMORIAM

Rudi Klein
1936–2001

DANKE, RUDI!

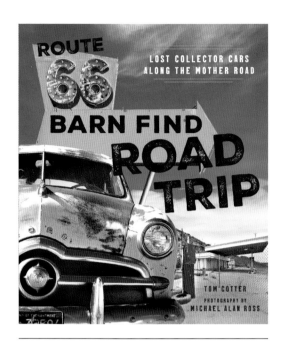

ROUTE 66 BARN FIND ROAD TRIP
978-0-7858-3749-7

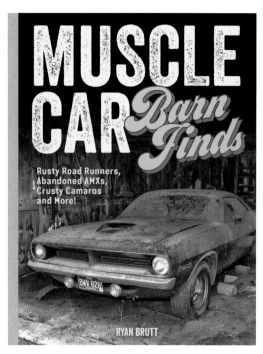

MUSCLE CAR BARN FINDS
978-0-7603-5359-2

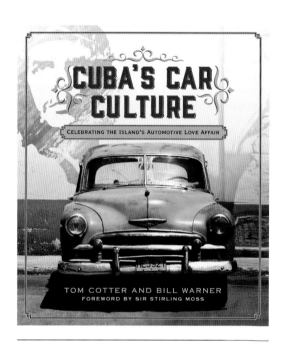

CUBA'S CAR CULTURE
978-0-7603-5026-3

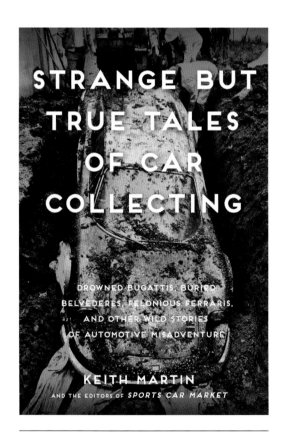

STRANGE BUT TRUE TALES
OF CAR COLLECTING
978-0-7603-5360-8

TOM COTTER'S BEST BARN-FIND
COLLECTOR CAR TALES
978-0-7603-6303-4

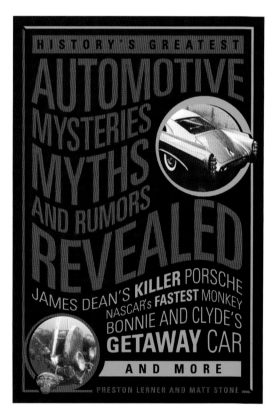

HISTORY'S GREATEST AUTOMOTIVE
MYSTERIES, MYTHS, AND RUMORS REVEALED
978-0-7603-4714-0